Airs, Waters, Places

KUHL HOUSE POETS   *edited by Jorie Graham and Mark Levine*

Airs, Waters, Places

Poems by Bin Ramke

University of Iowa Press ᴪ Iowa City

University of Iowa Press, Iowa City 52242
Printed in the United States of America

Design by Richard Eckersley

http://www.uiowa.edu/~uipress

The publication of this book was gener-
ously supported by the University of Iowa
Foundation.

Printed on acid-free paper

Library of Congress
Cataloging-in-Publication Data
Ramke, Bin, 1947–
Airs, waters, places: poems/by Bin Ramke.
p.   cm.—(Kuhl House poets)
ISBN 0-87745-776-X (pbk.)
I. Title. II. Series.
PS3568.A446 A68 2001
811'.54—dc21   2001027432

01 02 03 04 05 P 5 4 3 2 1

Again, for Nicolas and Linda

From these things he must proceed to investigate everything else. For if one knows all these things well, or at least the greater part of them, he cannot miss knowing, when he comes into a strange city, either the diseases peculiar to the place, or the particular nature of common diseases.

Hippocrates, *On Airs, Waters, and Places*

How, then, could blood ever turn into bone, without having first become, as far as possible, thickened and white? And how could bread turn into blood without having gradually parted with its whiteness and gradually acquired redness?

Galen, *On the Natural Faculties*

Contents

ACKNOWLEDGMENTS

The following journals published these poems:

American Letters and Commentary: "Surface Tension"; *American Review*: "Tiny Wounds: A Theory of Generosity"; the *Colorado Review*: "After Artemidorus on Dreams: *Oneicriticos*" and "Paraclete"; *Conjunctions*: "Gravity and Levity"; *Fourteen Hills*: "Against the Cycle of Saint Ursula (Carpaccio)"; the *Germ*: "Echo"; *Interim*: "Raise Grief to Music"; the *Ohio Review*: "The Science of Reunion and Opposition"; the *Paris Review*: "String"; *Quarterly West*: "Zoo," and "Uses of Reality"; *Western Humanities Review*: "On the Shape of Such as Planets, Like Earth"; and *forPoetry.com*: "Virtual Sculpture."

I am grateful also to individuals for generous readings and the inspiration of their own and various arts, including Jenny and Jorie and Donald and Rick and Brian and Cole and Bill.

Airs, Waters, Places

No Thing

A word that is almost deprived of meaning is noisy. Meaning is limited silence.
Maurice Blanchot

Sound as corruption is a further fall, a grace
like wind's incessant pounding, a music as anger—
air belligerent *versus* a single tree in a field
which is elegance as horizon as curtain drawn
against (any tree in singularity) light and light
whose nobility of patience penetrates the weather:
and from the air, from the airplane I saw
I saw beneath me during that time (I think it was time)
of year I saw the fall of leaves around each tree separate
a powdering of color pastel chalked circle a disk of leaves
and then red and bronze dots and then (we climbed)
the distant earth and then cloud and glitter
as soft in the distance like clouds among
cloud the tree speaking not to me only to itself like God.
Not silent. Nothing is. No thing like it except
surrounds itself with vibrating molecules
known as noise unless it is the susurrant leafage defiant
calling attention, calling. You recall, "Nothing
will come of nothing," said Lear to Cordelia.

After Artemidorus on Dreams: *Oneicriticos*

I could live there, a little hut in the right eye,
the great witch vanquished, Fermat restored
to health just long enough to face his own
narrow margin—the world of whim and wisdom,
home. In the forest. I would wander there
and bear arms, my father's souvenir revolver
in my hot child's fist, headed for heroic.

Or the one about the fate of nations,
the snake entwined in the viscera
of a dying deer—anyone's interpretation . . .

When I was depressed I would remember
Rolle's Theorem—I would recall the day
I stood at the blackboard where an ancient
mathematician smiled upon me—intricate
the ways of man, the manner of his deceit.

Enuknia: an unimportant dream—to some—
which would not tell the future. Some
sleep is not worth sleeping, some nights
are mere neglect of light, lingering.

Ephialtes: the nightmare. Consider the beasts,
how full of teeth their faces, how foul
the leaking breath. See them tear flesh—yours—
and drink the blood. Oh surely not real.

Chrematismos: which we need not distinguish
from *oraculum*, tells the future. And
why not? The hard problem, really, is the past.
Alas the long hallway, the turns and corridors
branching into what we could call "success,"
for instance, or "failure"—some such fulcrum
against which to push—or "parable": there was

a boy who worked all through the night cutting
cane from an infinite field who would sleep
through the day and dream of huge machinery
wiping wide swaths clear of sugar through
his night, then again would wake
to the dark to lift his own machete
and wearily work his way to morning,
to rest and random dark.

Oramo: vision of the future, clear, the kind
of thing to bet on—the horse to back
named and numbered. Such a dream
frightens everyone. Who knows what mind
can know the future thus well, this
willfully? —is too terrible to think upon.

Oneiros (the dream which requires interpretation):
all reality is virtual—here's no excuse for sadness
consider the starving the lilies
the children of the field who toil
neither are they happy

        walking home I
noticed the snow was general
and the smoke rose stiffly
from the houses, the warm interiors
locked safe from my vision
if not from inhabitants staring each
into her own space her own resonance . . . ,
what you are pleased to call pornography
an immersion of self beyond sincerity
preconscious flowering of possibility
a sacrament too dangerous to discuss:

        walking home I
noticed the sunlight slanted against
the bark of trees the texture complex
and the implications most astounding
the boiling of biology there

3

                    walking aimlessly I
watched the children concern themselves
with history and the clashing of nations
the casual arrogance of the political
they presciently persisted announcing
themselves and persisted in the economies
their sly exuberances and outlandish
little lives. And they were terrified.   St. Mark
After the fall of the temple what can matter?
For instance, mediocrity looms,

and old age shuffles after.   (You may already be a winner.)
"Now he whistles after the wind
and preaches sadness in sad tones."   (Nietzsche)
Aristotle thought of fossils as failed genesis,
attempts of life to struggle from the mud—*ad astra per
et cetera*—how lovely. I too believe it. And it is
so: merely reverse. Hold one in your hand, a shard
in the shape of a million years of fish,
and be frightened.

Watery

whatever is not cannot be
whatever is cannot not be
                    Anaxagoras

like love the river, no
not like but the river
fills itself, is full, cannot be other

is a river? the water?
full or perhaps empty if
a river is empty is there a river?

beautiful perhaps whether
or not it is, the river
aligned with the bank, lined by

the boundary limnal
fauna the wading birds
beaks shimmer with the river

dripping and the agony—
is it agony to die
a fish down the gullet of a heron?

is a heron beautiful? is
the heron part of the river?
what my mother

called a coulee, through
her childhood her town not
a town it was empty—

is there a town with no
people or dogs?
she and her family

tipped
into the river, the coulee,
their flat-bottomed barge

in the flood
a famous flood
where is the river the land covered

by water the depth
deceptive this
is what it is like to be beautiful

not like but to be
not beauty but necessity
not a river but water

not a heron but
like a heron, long beaked
and full of fish

not flying but wading
not happy but
home

"Without figure or fable"

Nietzsche admired Thales admiring clarity (water as father)
water as everything, in its way—the world. As if,
     as pre-Socratic as if my father were—
my father the chemist knew water taught me titration.
At age eleven I helped him analyze—phenolphthalein
released by drips into the swirling flask we admired the drama
of color change but kept my count cleverly—it is now winter
     far from the lakes of home, the likes of it.
Remember to cry, the clarity of crying,
or cryogenic—no, only frozen, snow only, it drifts
across our vision, it accumulates. Tears.
     Clarity is what we wanted most, lost nothing,

not simple—the sidewalks do glisten this evening,
the cars pass hissing after rain, after thaw.
  Their paired lights litter the walks what is there
to see but what we put there there are many
sources of light few of water   forty years before a father
  loved me in our conspiracy of clarity huddled watching
the color change, the light   shining through the tube
I learned to weigh the color of light against a chart—the shape
of a molecule of water
        is the shape of those pillows you watch TV
encircled by—reminiscent of a hug the oxygen in the center
        two hydrogen arms extended—
Here join, O welcome, Happy
        conjunction I sit in bed—
        the gray light laps at the window
the light is from the box the TV terrorizing
the center of the unclear the muddle of modern
        life after father, water, wandering fluid flow   hydrodynamics
        naval architecture
        hoses and drainpipes   gutters
storm drains city streets fountains
hydrants   monthly retention   micturation
        diuretic irrigation   rain   sleet
snow   drizzle   mist   hail
rainbow   glaze   steam   stream
river   lake   pond   rivulet   sea   bay
        ocean   gulf   canal   channel   dam
mill pond   bayou   coulee   reservoir   swamp
        marsh   the intracoastal waterway offers shipping protection across
the entire Atlantic and Gulf of
Mexico coast a length incalculable a defense

there is no defense

for instance: doll, clothed
hand mirror, tortoiseshell-backed—
spoons
cookery matters of various sorts—
well-seasoned Dutch oven et cetera

two brooms
an alarm clock, wound, damaged
too quickly to ring

and the full pathos of a small family
the laughter of waves, wavering
under the long nose of gar

the flat-eyed bass, the perch,
a thin fish, easy to catch
and then at Aswan

a kind of flood
preserved
entire the family tombs and titles

mother peers into the toilet bowl reads dark signs
messages from the interior   how many sources?
the breath   the color of urine
the false shapes   who does not accept
a message from anywhere

stars   home   viscera
whence they come, whither they go
mystery behind the flesh beneath the stretched
and sallow skin will kill us in the end, children

and there might have been happiness in the night
a mother-child conspiracy   a man I know
took rouge from the mortician's hand
and himself replaced the color in his dead mother's cheek
pushed the cotton wadding in to fill the hollows
oh gone and glittering mom into the boy's night
peering into the dark remains.

Zoo

                        who would
listen for what goes bump in the

goes boom in the morning a father

a man I know takes bombs apart for
a living bomb disposal being

a modern way to live with
fear   you

need merely be careful
my father said pay attention boom

in the night fire in the hole
another of those adult cold mornings

and the light is warily silver someone
feels better someone lives well

most delicate mode wish for the past
a past which with

care and cunning could be made to work
to order

this is a dream a past that works
as the present is an edge slicing

mind into sagital sections
as if

a formula   flies thrown through the
air arced   adhesion of

things attach to   fact   there is real
and there is not not   is a

difference   the imagined is a kind
of real   memory too

there was
a day I   was a small child

running among the legs of a father a grand
father   a brother   an uncle

I was praised for youth the war was over

nothing needed   exploding explaining
the tropical   the weeds of the pasture

the cows   distant   the future

distant   the line of trees   beyond
which the murk of water and cypress

knees rising   this was

and white egrets distant once
became hats   entire birds dead

to adorn   shot for two feathers

mon panache   it was a time
gone who cares

nothing to it

what child not me would
listen for what bump in the night

that goes boom in the morning

my father took bombs apart for the war
disposal being   a part of valor

a most modern way to
be careful my

father said   *pay your own way*   attention
in the night   fire in the hole

pain   not counting loneliness
a moment of terror for instance a sound of braking

and over the rise of the interstate one truck
turned sideways floating into your rearview mirror

a clarity a dialogue with self
in which the possible passes

this is not interesting
I thought that if I could put it all down, that would be one way.   John Ashbery

picture here

a cottage an adequate estate something
to live on pretty et cetera you cannot

see it to hear is possible the birds and some cows
lowing in the distance   slow sloe-eyed cows

in the distance

what (if a house be built beside
still water in the evening fowl descend

awkward in their way to settle raucously
walking on water then sinking comfortable

in their element) happens next no one
knows what happens next

the spectacular this evening
great streak of purple heavy against cold

golden light the result of refraction clouds
frame the event give it depth

in time at the moment   *(after all, who won*

of the light going the color   *the Peloponnesian War?*
deepens beyond bearing will

touch with such magnificence you feel   *and how many died?*
your own future collapse sweetly

                                                     . . . all of them
                                                     to tell the truth in time

Cows
are warm walls and patient

                                                     about the past find
try to remember the names   *its implication for the future*
lean your head against her flank   *anywhere but here*

the reverberating breath and the chewing   *now here nowhere*

the deepening din   *in time)*
that sound

the horns of a cow are one kind of danger
memory is the other

I would once I did I could   make as we say
love and she was   there among the two

of us   It was a world   and home or might

as well have been   to climb limbs
like that to insert the self   in flesh

to live as if we were not   dying in tandem could
we   did we

what memory will do to the past   is too funny
for words

there are pleasures   a clean light intrudes

there are ways to know

you have felt it usually pain   it was harder

to be a child than anyone knew   you were
who wasn't   it fell through him

I should have remembered the war it happened
two years before my birth

a stronger mind would remember   dismembering
the crustaceous whose arrogant apathy

fills the void what armed creature
this was was recalled   called to the boy

she stood in the doorway   the boy did not heed
hear   she loved him he   remembers her his mother

a shadow   a map of me
on the world the wall one dimension   lost

Suddenly everything is beautiful. He begins to cry   Russell Edson
because it hurts   because it doesn't

the numbers don't add up   or they do
because Mom should be sent

to a home   because she refuses to go
because she smears the good rug

with dung   perhaps her own   perhaps the dog's
because there is a war

13

because there is no war   which would teach the young
"life"   that it's hard and

political   During the Second World War
the zoo in Tokyo starved

its animals   what recourse
what if Americans bombed

liberated lions elephants like cows
would wander the footpaths

the theory of everything says   some things are continuous
some are discrete   contentment

is knowing the difference
if there is a difference

nothing is what it used to be   or is
the sunset is not fleeting

it is continuous and absolute   the only one
the one which has been happening

ever since the earth solidified out of a ring

of debris   even before that the ring
of debris refracted sunlight

into constituent wavelengths
including the ultraviolet   the infrared

which we so want to see it is just there beyond the edge
if the world hates you

know that it has hated me   John 15:18
before you   if the world

loves you you're on your own
"After clinging to their foreclosed chicken ranch

for two years, two women gave up the fight
and killed themselves and all their pets

just before the marshals seized the property"   Associated Press
For a week the undiscovered bodies lay

in the garage. Thelma
J. Lee, 67, and Maureen R. O'Boyle, 51,

asphyxiated   three dogs on the floor twelve cats
in the pickup   one in a shopping cart   *What would happen if bombs*
                                                    hit the zoo? If the cages were broken
In a Japanese picture book   *and dangerous animals escaped*
children would pass and the elephants   *to run wild through the city . . .*
                                                    By command of the Army, all
stretched trunks through the bars begging   *of the lions, tigers*
anything it is forbidden to feed   *leopards, bears, and big snakes*
                                                    were poisoned.
no one is forgiven   Yukio Tsuchiya, *Faithful Elephants*

"It is generally accepted that the domestication of cattle followed sheep, goats, pigs and
dogs. Modern domestic cattle evolved from a single early ancestor, the aurochs. . . . It is
believed the last surviving member of the species was killed by a poacher in 1627 on a
hunting reserve near Warsaw, Poland."

                                        okstate.edu, *"Breeds of Livestock"*

Tiny Wounds: A Theory of Generosity

I. *Traum, Trauma*

Because it was the year she was happy, she kept always near
dictionaries published in 1943;
verträumen her time away like a German grandmother
into the plausibility of what is called
in English, A Happy Childhood—of the night her mother died
she dreamed of fire
and the clean light gleaming off the desert, the sort of place
you see from the train
on the way to San Diego after New Orleans
to see your father before he ships
out for the Pacific, a dream in white above the gunwales.

She never believed in dreams, never remembered them, or if she did wouldn't con-
fess. She borrowed mine to take to her doctor, laughed at me, my flat, thin life, so
unlyrical and usual spilling so stilly into anyone's hands, her expectations. But it
was something to share, and it made me believe she loved me. When it was my turn
it seemed to me wrong to use again those same dreams, so I thought up new ones
to beguile myself.

II. Cannibal Necessity

What kind of normalcy to spend hours each week
kneeling before a statue of a near-naked man, the sex
emphasized by drapery, this man bleeding profusely
or perhaps drained already of blood through five piercings
plus the head, the tender flesh of the face a lyrical
laceration? It was called *passion*, and was what we knew of God.

God was invented by the Greeks, of course, or some such
race of preliterate pirates, full of vicious sympathy and
piercing contemplation of the species to come, the generously,
profusely mortal meanings of being human. Whoever could invent

sex and sin, delirium and dream, such a creator could have prevented
weak-willed cruelty if it had wanted. But here we are, and remain,

remains being one word for corpse; but whatever was it
prevented us from dining on our selves and neighbors,
inventing rules to separate ourselves from the soil, the fertile if
generously vicious rock and rotting ground we walked on upright full of
sympathy and agony, arrogance and apathy, all the accoutrements
such biology gave us, such a nature we hide from?

III. Other Languages

She would speak as if to herself or no one, anyone
listening could not know (no fair
weather friends, whether or not)   *she also collected*
to whom she addressed such   *guidebooks, ancient*
silences laced with laughter.   *and modern*
Nothing is funny, but everything
makes her laugh. Otherwise she is as normal as anyone,
and as happy. The past crumbles, or was it a page
from her diary
yellowed, even a map?
She was once small and   *the weather remains*
needing to know something, tried traveling.   *weather, fair and*
Prague, Budapest, Bucharest, all   *warm enough*
the rest. Money lasts longer she says.   *everywhere*
American money. In foreign parts.
And you can always ask for more. Anywhere.
Sometimes they give it.

[*der Edelmut*, no, is wrong. Is about arrogance, noblesse
oblige, to use another other-tongue; *der Grossmut*, (what is
this *mut*—mood? As if the recognition of one's kind,
being one with the species, were a matter of mood?)
because she thought that, that to be generous was
to see the self in others, to recognize our common
ancestors, to become one instead of many. How strange
of her, to fail to fear the stranger. She was wrong.]

Uses of Reality

                Do we yes
we love everyone once, anyone
forever—as the price of the
fleeting
                other versions:
Narcissus doomed to self-knowledge
hangs his unhappy head over
the pool's
                edge, in desperation
dying a hunger artist un-
happy unhoping while poor
Echo
                turns invisible be-
coming only bone and landscape
only speaking when spoken to
rapt
                pupil of every passing
fool and repeated repeating
every line a lingering
what is
                the poem if not the
response to any who opens
the book and imposes
a self
                there, reposes; listen,
my words come back like good dogs
I whistle and the poem unfolds
a kind
                of pose, a kindness exposed,
. . . is a story a sequence a word
and a word and yet still the pool
reflects
                the face of posed Narcissus
he is knowledge he is Adam
he is home alone; *what*

demarcates
      this category of
patient is despair and futility—
their lives feel permanently empty.
They
      cannot use reality.
      Glasser, 1992
Otherwise anyone can play;
"———!" he caroused, or cautioned,
knowing
      it was his last word
eloquented himself to himself,
mindfully, wispishly,
as if
      his own reflection were
sufficient reason to
live this way, leave this way,
die,
      evil or vile
beneath the wavering V of geese
carried away, away, his face
inches
      away from the reflecting
surface of the pool a sufficient
world an air an edge of air and
light
      and so we use yes.

Against the Cycle of Saint Ursula (Carpaccio)

How Saint Ursula, born of royal blood and given the most religious upbringing in the faith of our Lord Jesus Christ, consented to be bride to the son of the king of the Angels[sic], Pagano; and how, accompanied by eleven thousand virgins, she came to Rome; how with them all Pope Ciriacus set out from Rome with many Holy Bishops and betook him to Cologne where, on arrival, they were all killed, women and men, for their constancy in their faith.

> Jacopo da Voraigine, *Golden Legend*, edited by
> Nicolo Malerbi, printed in Venice by Jenson, 1475

Arrival of the English Ambassadors to the Court of the King of Brittany

If you must begin with the visual then imagine the weedy line
along the fence, the fence a manifestation of order, the weeds
saved from the mower blade by the wire, the shape
of land enclosed as geometrical as a measured earth allows.

What do I love? besides the very earth.

As geology rises imagination fails. People live. And dogs.
That summer the other boys talked to me of the calculus; they laughed behind my back
as I struggled at integration, but you could tell they were shaky with the concept themselves.
We stayed up late whispering of the algorithms to come, of computers and new types
of proofs hidden within. Again they laughed at my desire for isolation
and the glittering grandeur of primes.

Paul, the rug merchant, showed us his videos of Turkey,
all the young girls glittering in the heated room
the floors a flourish of scarlet and medallions
a door opened briefly and the same sun as the American
shone on the spidery looms

a glitter of agony, of long sufferance, of ardor.
If Paul is a good man, he is also a merchant
and his art is not the same as the girls'.

L'Arrivo degli ambasciatori inglesi presso il re di Bretagna: as is so often the case in these fifteenth-century works, the detail is heartbreaking—the dog in the street, the small group of five tiny over the shoulder of the delegate, the full shape of sail smooth as the underside of a breast. The hips of that gondolier.

The Departure of the English Ambassadors from the King of Brittany

Ambitious to be eccentric, we were pleased to maintain distance and
nurture our peculiarity, or at least a solitude intriguingly sweet,
a solace during hot afternoons when she nervously avoided our soiled
raised hands which would soon drop defeated. The cascade of books
continued as if offstage but the librarian in History shyly kept his eyes
on his own page. *What are you doing in my century?* said the substitute,
easy in her anger. Simple variations like any enigma end with faith
or love, stories to God. These were her demesne. Maybe
a stage such as children go through.

Distraction is our constant condition. See how big the known can grow
in the simply human: see America on the old maps, how Cuba fills the
Caribbean while *terra incognita* shrinks upstaged.

Like birds they rise into the sky they fly

(*Il Commiato degli ambasciatori inglesi*)

Return Home of the English Ambassadors

Saint Augustine reported his dream: a child   Nomé, 1623
on a beach (we had no beach mudflats dark and
organic not here green light and parallels)
the child pouring buckets of seawater into a hole in the sand   a task
a meaningful sandfull of gesture the axiom   Monsu Desiderio of Naples
made little pictures we didn't know his name he knew us well enough
sinister clarity   abridged not
necessarily true   the dream of Saint Augustine
more beautiful than anything   the child pouring water
into a hole in the sand

there was a message, this dream was readily interpreted to refer to the dogma of the Trinity, such a big deal they made of it, such a fuss over fusion of the family, leaving out Mom of course, into the masculine we go. . . .

(They promise to build a bridge even when there is no river.
Nikita S. Khruschev)

The writer must increase the sum of liberty in the world—in this Sartre was correct. Like any antientropist, one who calls himself *literary* must take on the not-merely-problematic-but-impossible task. Which can only be accepted blindly, with a sort of giggle, by the feeble. (Virtue is its own reward, vice earns its way.)

There is a monkey eyeing a guinea hen in this picture, protecting what he holds in his hand. What does he hold in his hand? More subtle than any child.

(Rimpatrio degli ambasciatori inglesi)

Meeting of Ursula and Ureus and Departure of the Pilgrims

So I had a life handed me and I lived it.　　All order distorts; incoherence is one accuracy:　　*Incoherence seems to me preferable to a distorting order.*

Roland Barthes

I want to fix for a moment my sense of connection to the world. To call language a nervous system might be useful: if each sentient being is analogous to cells within the organism, language is analogous to the nerves as well as the messages sent along those nerves. There is, there, if not eternity, at least delusion.

He experienced both bliss and horror in contemplating the way an inclined line, rotating spokelike, slid upwards along another, vertical one—in an example illustrating the mysteries of parallelism.

The American mind terribly aware of itself

there are geometries beyond the body
(the attribute of St. Agatha is a plate of breasts severed)
severe resistance
the story is

F. O. Matthiessen

But with the aid of a ruler he forced them to unlock: he simply redrew them, parallel to one another, and this gave him the feeling that out there, in infinity, where he had forced the inclined line to jump off, an unthinkable catastrophe had taken place. . . .

Vladimir Nabokov, The Defense

(*L'Incontro dei fidenzati e partenza in pellegrinaggio*)

It is the whole world entire smaller climbing the hillside (called perspective but we know it really does get smaller, the world, as it climbs) and the various size ships in the lagoon waiting, wind filling (wind pushing against therefore pressing into a shape of a segmented arc) the sails. A half-moon shape; hemisphere.

The Dream of St. Ursula

Only when no one uses a word anymore is that word available to the writer

such as the word "remember," last used by Robert Duncan in this sentence in 1964: "The sinister children at table reject their food, / spewing up bits, / member by member remember."

A poem can prevent onrushing light going out. Narrow path in the teeth of proof. Fire of words will try us. Grace given to few. Coming home through bend and bias for the sake of why so. Awkward as I am. Here and   there invincible things as they are.

Susan Howe

the saint lies chastely in bed (I lie this way too—straight, facing the ceiling, sheets neatly tucked around me) a (the right) hand to her ear as if in her dream to hear the angel the angel in the doorway (or at least against a source of light in that the shadow disappears before her) the angel with symbolic accoutrements the saint dreams meanwhile the room is so tidy and there centered facing us is another pet dog small but courageous and unperturbed being a dog.

Surely beneath the bed of a saint is a chamberpot. It is so human to think so.

(*Il Sogno della santa*)

23

Meeting of the Pilgrims with Pope Ciriacus by the Walls of Rome

    Lightning in the mountains
the rumble and bang and distance,
the hope delicious that you will
not be killed, but the thrill, the pattern
and aggression.
There is honor to be salvaged, and
you can be alone.

Avert your eyes. The thunder throws
itself from one mountain to the other
and still it is not the end of the world.
It need only happen that one morning
the sun not rise—on such a morning
search for consolation like a little
yellow sun on the edge and not yet
the end but you can see the pattern.

(L'Incontro dei pellegrini con papa)

Arrival of the Pilgrims at Cologne

It makes us sad and we go to bed without dinner.
"I have been grateful for my store:
Let me say grace when there's no more"
                    Robert Herrick, "To God in Time of Plundering"
She mourns the self she could have been
whose spidery parentlike wisdom—
a future equal to the past as if nothing
could happen only once. To prove
her head unbroken she counted
backward for the nice policeman. She failed
and filled her heart with grief for the past
she a small woman alone now, in a strange landscape.

(L'Arrivo a Colonia)

24

Martyrdom of the Pilgrims and Funeral Rites of St. Ursula

"No one hates the mirror which reflects his face,"
said the man whose mother was beautiful.
Then he returned his change to the cabby, his
tip through the crystal coffin between them,
comfortable bullet proofing. But it's raining
like movies, the street gleaming, the windows
fogged, and a faceless form waits impatient
on the curb. Another kind of angel, a sense
of mortality like the TV image
the ghost of the weatherman, of the whole
world's weather: "Did I ask for forgiveness
when Mother brought me home
from the hospital to voices susurrant, un-
relenting as wallpaper? I could see radio
waves wavering through my room
on their way to Moscow or Omaha,
the clever horizon bending light gravely
past the setting sun.
If only there were a word for it."

NOT THE EXPRESSION of clean disgust,
shit as in merde, but the thing itself
the interiority expressed, pressed into the world
my grandfather homeless would Learlike move
among his daughters' houses a month or so to each
carrying with him a bedpan unaccustomed as he would be
to the new routes those nights to the bathrooms.
In the morning the twentieth-century daughter
would clean the remains of her father.

It is our remaining attachment
to the unredeemed and the persistent,
unclean as mortality, beyond redemption.

(Il Martirio dei pellegrini e funerali della santa)

Exaltation of St. Ursula and of Her Companions

In the machinery of injustice
my whole being is Vision.

> Susan Howe

The strangeness of a strange name cut
from the moorings of association: the word
and the wildness of it all context. *Siam*
will no longer do. And the rug, even were it
to fly, can no longer be from Persia.

"I have never been anywhere and I plan
to stay home. My mother traveled once
during the war from Washington D.C.
to San Diego to see my father who,
by the time she arrived dragging my
brother by the hand and swollen full
with me, had sailed into the furious
archipelago of unexploded ordnance,
the alien Asian seas; O adventurous, my father,
and dutiful, fuses and trinitrotoluene
filling his dreams. I like best in life

a good park in spring and the greenness
flowers, too, and always young mothers
to push babies in spindly machines
the delicate boredom to sit in the shade
to watch and to hum soft loops and whorls
like a fine hand, a practiced hand. Writing."

The hand writing on the wall or the hissing
can of spray. Language abhors a blank wall.
His art did express
A quintessence even from nothingnesse.

> Donne

In a book who wrote: "Boredom is the dream bird
that hatches the egg of experience"
and then he traveled famously
from Germany during that war
and died by his own hand untimely?

"Yesterday after rain the sun caused a forsythia
to steam, the coolness of the mountain air
and the ultraviolet rays. I expected voices.
The immense effort of Nature is disturbing,
you want to offer it a day off or something.
Anyway I watched a snake-shaped cloud
invade the valley this morning, between
two peaks floating all full of dignity.
The sleepiness below—it *was* early—and lonely.
The trunks of aspen columnar against the sky
are black, but ghostly pale against the mountains.
The dark, wet earth after the storm."

(*Apoteosi della santa*)

Paraclete

"I am concerned in these my later years
with the origin of things; I am become a simple lover."
And who disagrees disagrees discreetly; who would
wound such a person, such a program?
This is a world to him: water, earth, air, ambition.
This is how it works: an interior tryst, a private
agreement with himself to love it all always, its charm.
"I will call it my Paraclete, my paramour;
I will be a faithful suitor, persistent and mild
to the end—I will be the Man Who Loved the World."
He was a man without a childhood
born into the void. In his dreams he enacts
a kind catastrophe—who could do other?
He folds the blank sheet of "life so far"
into a toy to sail exuberantly yet
he knows nothing of aeronautics,
a man of passion such as this is,
a man of words and fearsome folly.

Raise Grief to Music

Louis Zukovsky

The erotic dimension of grief includes
any anguish, a calm dissolution, an orderly
denial, a convergence of agonies, a diffidence—
                    it has its geometries.

Some live this way afterward: the sun
shining on the wicked, and the cold
glimmer all any former child recalls.
Sing Aha! Exclaim it. A full
urgency loud as cascading ice
the implicating weather. I see it,
weather happens whoever's dead
and the light so just so when she
stands against the light her
dress and draperies diaphanous
interior

Someone tell the neighbors someone
drink to her life in the light. My
life hath been one love—no blot it out
My life hath been one chain
of contradictions Madhouses Prisons
wh-re shops—never doubt But
that my life hath had some strong
convictions That such was
wrong, John Clare,
Poems of the Epping Forest
I want to live in Italy.

I want neighbors who love me
and leave me alone. I want
to be happier than you.
I am grateful for the world's small
kindnesses I would kill
to keep them. This is one

when the present
becomes tissue-thin
I try to remember
ambition, mine,
anyone's
to be immortal.
Only the flight
of birds comes to mind
patterned shape in terror
wilderness—the wisdom
some would call it—
I watch through the
pane
on such a day my face
against, the breath as I speak
to myself the words freeze
adhering—outside is snow
and green of certain trees—
abies, for instance *concolar*
violacaea, a blue light
beneath the white, *box*
across the lawn,   *micriphylla,*
turning brown, catalpas
shedding leaves quickly as
rain, quietly.
Breathed onto
the pane breath hardens how
like a life how small—homely
the second snow of winter,

way to live. It is so sad it is
morning. To the cynical all
is theory after all. And
in the trees are birds
singing each to each
not to us.

Afterward anyone
can say anything and will
do so   so doing desire
more attention; attend to the flowers,
pansies for instance through snow
cheap and plentiful, plenitude
a partial embrace, a solace

something shines
after the funeral, waxed
a gleam black long
flashing in all weathers
the gash of ground aghast

among the griefs
a leaf, snow as foreign
they live foreignly, The Dead,
far from anticipation

of grief   O Mom
O Dad   refuge
from a formal anxiety of grief
home a place of grieving
home as

embrace the necessary, she said
as if she knew.   She
chose a handful of dirt to toss
with grace onto the coffin—not
everyone knows how.

nothing to remark—she breathed
onto the pane the words O, O
small moaning vocatives afterward
can be scraped with the fingernail—
Ice. Slip of the tongue,
brave device.

Time *does* pass.

A most common
emblem of time—of danger, of death,
of grief, of age—the hourglass
a version of earth
dripping—yes, let's say
hour glass, crystalline
container of abstraction
inexorability—Kampyle
of Eudoxus, you'll recall, is
a famous curve suggestive
of the classic shape of the hour
glass—its Cartesian formula
$a^2x^4 = b^4(x^2+y^2)$
a polar form is available
for those more comfortable
among the conic sections)

Eudoxus, ungrateful
pupil of Plato, famous
for inventing the astrolabe,
famous (as we once would say,
immortalized)
for describing constellations
famous for introducing
mathematical astronomy
to the Greeks, famous
as the first (imagine it, being
such a first in a long line)
to mean the word: *constellation*,
tumbling into time.

The Gods That Sleep in Museums

Jorie Graham

It is cool and guarded. Godly.
The children are killing each other elsewhere
not here not among the marble busts and cenotaphs.

Under cover of daylight the dawn cowers—it is
only light innocent as anything a veil of seeing against
the glare of godliness the good like anger and
there is the integrity of shadow to annoy—there is
nothing for it in time this time of day—the dare.

A small mass of children seethes down
the street downhill hissing and spitting its way
past the louvered windows and shuttered
the small mass like cancer grows—No it is
only children otherwise called not history but

I have met a new and beautiful woman and
therefore the world makes a different sense
this morning she wears pearls a stringed instrument an
assortment of small smooth stones—she could
throw them the string could break the small
organically induced calcium deposits could
clatter like laughter onto the marble floor
small arcs degrading over time (bounce).

Eggs eyes riverstones rough roundness
of boulder gems cut and uncut

In a new calculation of risk we must
cast what small stones lie at hand
lying being the better part of valor
and fear being worse than fidelity bad as
bones—wings are another option cool and moist
unfolding gluey from the furred backs of moths
emerging into dark from the light of their soft eggs.

Somewhere in Gaza a boy opens both eyes

to the coming of the Prophet and grasps
a smallish stone igneous formed in
volcanic exuberance—to be the first the boy
to cast carefully this his small vote
against the national interest—his god
a small gnawing a dark egg of danger
which boys love boys live for like anything they do.

So here's the first lesson of history: hide.

The arc of each thrown stone confers
inevitability the tiny dance of fate the look
of numerical necromancy—once the stone leaves
the hand of the boy thrown in high spirit
a high arc a heraldry of itself

the stone is only acted upon is an agent of other
but might as well be its own universe it
falls fatal and full of significance

no god could be better served they clatter
small stones in the street the museum is shuttered

we are so lucky there is nothing called the past
we are so lucky we are a stone god is
another word for luck—for stone—for fear
the museum is the last refuge of refuge
it loves the little light the peace

the movement of stone upon stone
is a kind of burning.

Surface Tension

Consider the tear, the silver dis- solution of self into salt and
water—that is me down my cheek, turning cold on my collar.
Or there, in that corner, the child who weeps machinelike no doubt
in pain but small, harmless pain. Not mine. But is. Tearful and fond
of his own small world, himself examining his happy past
lost, a twin, a sort of twin.

Reflection is predictable beauty. Doubling into symmetry,
bilateral or sometimes bizarre. In mirrors. Car hoods.
On the terrazzo which the crew has splashed who now caress
with their succulent mops. Or a lake when there is little wind
and a world slowly waves to us smiling like relatives in the rear-
view mirror, glad to see us going. Or the accidental encouragement
the city offers, its wind eyes flashing us back at ourselves,
encouraging, reminding the boy who delights (endures) in the moment.
Clean windows. Glass to keep the world in place. The rain
outside. The Boy in. In the window

the lamp behind you floats into the infinite dark, and your
own face of course doubled, the window mirroring, the night.
The day will rise, the blonde twin, the favored one, will dull
the mirroring glass and dim the hovering lamp. It means nothing.

Here: think of a girl standing
in a lake—a litter of leaves surrounds her, she is reading
the pages a book in her one hand she is doubled—wavery—radiating—her
legs might be cold she wears a dress the hemline
above the water the girl reads what she believes—she reads herself
into a kind of love she is doubled she is inconsolable.
Those are not tears on the page those are tears on the page. Water
marks. Shadows. Those are tears on the page. That is a splash
of water—the lake the clinging world in one of its forms. Liquid.
The girl the earth the lake is like— a tear. You see through
a film of water, tears, vision depends upon the bathing of
the world in light, the eye in water.

People touch and between them is a   layer of darkness a thin skin of no-
light keeping them apart. A world.   To touch is to darken the space
between. The tear is bright, it   glistens, is a lens—the tear
is the girl in light   and the shape the world takes.

The Science of Reunion and Opposition

The weight of this sad time
we must obey: Speak
what we feel, not what   *King Lear*
we ought to say. Or not;
whatever is said is so. The world's in flames again.
Rain tonight, and tomorrow fills with
anguish and the body with enigmas, as when
"Aha, its whole, its seventh   *the Rhind Papyrus*
it makes nineteen" (. . . *aha, once thought*
to be hau, meant 'heap,' and was used
to denote the unknown in the problem).   Graham Flegg
Conundrums and the shining solutions
little paths through the woods and wisdom:
the difference
between evolution and entropy.
Childhood recollection and it was
my childhood, not yours.
The trope of contrivance   *trep*: to turn,
cleverly retrieved like any trophy,   zero-grade
a tropical creature   *tropos*, turning
treed and zooed, shooed home,
dark again and wet.

The world is flames again. Nineteen sixty-seven
we were young and in something like love, something
curious and we were clever. What happened then?
Some were dying—war. Some were dying—disease.
Some of us were delirious with what is sometimes
called *freedom*, sometimes *youth*—sometimes *evil*. God
was another word for it, and peril. Calculation.
Stony sleep. The long night ahead fills
with rain, lyrically off the roof drains. The color of
water of moon light which was fleeting they

drank to the one
forgetting the names of his heroes
and of his cousin in Argentina.
Stony sleep. The world in flames again:
Heraclitean dazzle and delirium again
how it looks all dead and all full of stars
or of pinholes and the light littering there
telling a story telling all (it's time
to turn the record) telling stories
like any boy who doesn't know much, show
and tell, sound and vision and voice of dream: *algebra becomes*
view occluded, it will be morning   *you, wears like*
he said gambling is like work   *any lingering*
on the assembly line pulling that handle again   *doubt or discipline*
and again . . . living in a boy's book anyone can
be heroic making silence into a clear preference
a decision as if the very air had itself to blame
silent masses move across the land, bridged—no
they made a noise the wind announced pleasure
music as his very breath: Speak
what we feel, not what we ought to say
the weight of this sad time we must obey.
God was another word for it, and peril.
(I lived there, you can take
my word for it. Among the bayous, sometimes
in little houses. They were happy, the Others,   *who could number*
or so they seemed to me who was ashamed.   *the stripes of the lilies,*
They danced and sang, they ate   *& observe the sparrow*
impudently, and died from time   *his range and reckoning*
to time and sang at their own funerals.
All appalling and nowhere to hide.
He, that particular one, fished for a living
and bribed small boys to talk to him.
His words were large and lingering
and his daughters dreaded his visits,
would grimace and mark the weeks.
I did believe all I heard, and half
of what I saw. I did pray that way,

and the sound of my own small whisper
shook the stained shards in their leadings;
no one else can hear this, and you are complicit)
what we ought to say
the weight of this sad time

The long night ahead fills
with rain, lyrically
off the roof drains

and someone solved my problems
like Fermat, like the coloring of maps,
like the efficient routes of postmen all
through the parish. Long ago and far, a foreign
feeling (al-Khwarizmi, the bone setter, the barber,
the linear unknown, the Königsberg bridge),
reason for the few and magic for the many
Egyptian, Babylonian and Greek algebra before Diophantus
was all largely rhetorical. We do find traces of what we would
term "syncopated" notation in the Egyptian mathematical
papyri, but it is purely arithmetic except in the case of the
hieratic symbol used to denote "heap". . . .
Sometimes abbreviations of the ordinal numbers were used
for unknowns. . . . We also find abbreviations of words denoting
fruit, flavours, and jewels

Flegg

The world is flames again, piled high.
Staying home nights
. . . instead of bullets wrapped in fire,
To make a shaking fever in your walls,

They shoot but calm words folded up in smoke,
To make a faithless error in your ears.

King John

Happy at home, and calm the evening comes

The Lord hath chastened me sore; but
he hath not given me over unto death

Psalm 118: 18

There are such people who live in one place

a lifetime, who know the territory
such people know a different world for its sameness
or mourn the passing of every moment

agonies abound, and burdens increase
none live so long, all must, once, cease
pause and refrain, both the same

because
we lived near one ocean, one ocean
was enough. Because we lived far

You can't persuade
a philosopher against
his will; but you may
feel a wind of doctrine
blowing through his
defenses against him.
George Santayana

from mountains, mountains were strange
because we lived with ourselves, ourselves
estranged who knew and know

we would conduct ourselves according
to the rules, we would bleed when spoken to,
answer when cut, we would walk

in curious circles in imitation of our own blood—
oh we would, and will again. The world
is again on fire and no one can deny us refuge
if we ask. The world is flames again, piled high.

"In my hypothetical body I linger
longer than you would believe possible.
I feel it, you know—you think I don't
but I do. Every time you speak
it touches me. The air, the molecular dis-
turbance, the way the very grass
trembles with each whispered syllable,
it all affects me and it hurts. Your silence
would cost you nothing. You have never suffered
like this you will never end my torture."

call it
what you will

Further evidence: *Angel* as
imaged in Western Tradition must be based
on the entomological model—not the segmented body
so much as the three paired appendages.
No vertebrate works this way.
And do they bleed?

(cut)

And what will I do if I finally achieve
a body of my own? Live in its shadow?
Beg its indulgence when I wish to be left
to my own devices, when I do NOT wish
to extend so vulgarly into the world,
the room, to displace the air so rudely?
What is the dark if not the warning
against which we wildly wave
our little hands like antennae
dreading the crushing weight of wisdom,
of absurd logic and laughable necessity.
It is a hopeless case, and I disclaim it.
I am such a burden to me, so homemade
and so necessary. I would sigh if I had breath.
I would bleed. It is burning
in the distance.

If I had bones to break, it would mend them
If I had numbers to puzzle, it would delude them
into submission, it is such a world
such a speculative ambition.
All is in flames, and we wish it so.
All is flame, and wishes. So.

conduct ourselves
to the rules
according

(It astonished me, the
way he poured
any leftover wine
on his cake.)
                    Daniel Cory

Virtual Sculpture

There is no excuse for sadness consider
the starving the lilies the children of the field
who toil not neither are they happy.

She is one who brings the weight
of industrial ingenuity to bear on a small
object of art.

She is open to the world's suggestion
she will declare it when she sees it she selects
metal objects to subvert General Motors
into art foundering she places the cast-off part
on a stone itself ecstatically chosen she
declares all is art in her small yard and I admire
the lines of silhouette, the delicate rust, the lingering there.

If she is also pregnant then she is two
and haunted by the opposite of ghost, the too
too solid and consider the tiny ocean there
the calm water less ocean than pool in which
the reflections of her face and flesh grow daily
Narcissus as mom, is, it is called expecting.

Is the future written in that pool which has
no surface a hand writing her hand or its it's
a found art a foundling castaway soon from its private
ocean, cast eros sore loser out.

Walking aimless I watched the children concern
themselves with history and the importuning of nations
no the casual arrogance of the world I noticed
the sunlight slanted against the bark of trees
the texture complex and the implications astounding
the boiling of biology along each limb a sculptural
announcing of itself the flesh the form the shape
casting the world and breaking the mold.

Moths and the Occasional Dog

Someone's telephone ringing in the distance—
a sound of traffic like some ocean—wind in trees et
cetera, closer—the occasional dog—*Siehe, ich lebe.*

I love Rilke because German is not English but almost
and I hide again and again in translations each
an obvious failure each providing room for me, Reader.

Reading a burning book turning the tinder page
at night by the light of the burning book reading
nothing burns like paper like nothing alive.

A little cluster of words to arrange—
house, school, church, a village, see how
the lights glow through painted windows.

(A bottle in the medicine cabinet
is labeled "hope" but none of us
is fooled all who can read know better.)

False fronts like western towns in the movies
behind which a duplicate reality lies
the difference is lighting—erotic to pornographic.

Seduction to delivery—the brightness of the room
and the color of its light will change or
the neon sign blinks in on

the lovers, sometimes blue,
sometimes bathed in blood
it would appear, if we could see.

Echo

Zoom

As if with the speed of sound,
as if it were fast, now we know
any schoolchild knows how quick the lightning
how lumbering the thunder . . .
and yet and yet

Yet It Bleeds

Who hears, who can hear, has ears.
And a voice is almost a vision, a form
a fair compromise: it was a good story and is told
again and again of a kind of anorexia, a nymph
purified by love for Narcissus, turned poet, turned
into voice, turned into mirror, mindless? Mindful
of sorrow, of shape, of solitude raptured.

Xenogamy

Bot. Pollination of the stigma of a flower
by pollen from a flower on another plant. [*xeno*,
alien, strange, guest, + *gámia*, to marry]
"Stigma": the eyespot of a protozoan, Greek
for tattoo, the mark of a slave.

Wounded

Unable to fly, a furious failing haunting her,
the creature in the garden evoluted a path
a circle breaking out of itself large
and larger, spiraling as if the self were escapable,

having failed, having fallen, bird self from the sky,
into an alienness full of fortune.

Verandah

Some such point-of-view—you know those areas
along the highway, "point of interest," "wildlife
viewing area," "point of geological interest,"
officially labeled by the highway department,
the CIA, who knows—those places where
the populace is invited to look at the world.
Some are indoors—the Mint, for instance,
where the delightful view of tons of copper pennies
flowing behind inch-thick glass is a reason
for children to leave the school to spend
an hour's viewing. What is it about?
Leisure? Memory is superfluous, a hindrance
annoying as history—what's there to see
except everything? Here, let's pull over,
the sun is setting again and we will regret it
tomorrow.

Unus + Versus, ppl. of vertere, to turn

This Land Darkened

Káthodos, descent, fall (of the soul): "The origins of the figure of the fall or banishment
of the soul from its natural, immortal abode are religious, as appears from its first
occurrence among the philosophers in Empedocles' *Purifications* (fr. 115; it may
have been held in some form by Heraclitus as well; see frs. 62, 68; Plato, *Gorg.* 492e–
493b; Plotinus, *Enn.* iv, 8, 1) where the banishment is the result of a primal crime
(bloodshed or flesh-eating; frs. 136, 137, 139) committed by one of the *daimones* (q.v.)
whose natural lot was immortality."

F. E. Peters, *Greek Philosophical Terms*

Sad Parades

"Self, for instance, me—"
he said slowly, languishing under the summer's
onslaught, reaching toward his remaining ambition
as if it were shimmering in someone's sight,
political being the term under discussion,
an ambition *versus* responsibility.
A story was boiling under them similar to
the one already dissipated, the cloud tattering
its own edges into oblivion. Sweetly.

Resolution Replies

Until finally the stars drift across our bedroom
over the bed and we are elsewhere and the stars
are themselves and the dark universe broods
upon its little Eggs and Wonders.

Quintessence Even from Nothingnesse

John Donne

For the stars to appear on *this* side of the window,
that they continue to be the nuclear machines they are
churning with violent intent but tiny, touchable.
That if we crept from bed we would trap them
by quietly shutting the window. That my brother
would continue to sleep. That the clouds would
accumulate as usual until morning, alas.

Perhaps It Is So

And look how dense the flesh, you can't
pass your hand through it it touches.

O

Who is gone?
Ora pro nobis.

Narration as Equivocation

"The moment I must remember was when
Into my clothes—every buttonhole filled with blue—
She twined flowers—what could they have been?—
(Yes, they were blue, and small, and too
Readily at hand) they were the color of eyes,
We tell of such betrayals—the postman arrived, me
(But let's assume such a memory is the lie)
Leaning away from her, she absorbed fully in the tree-

Like blossoming of the shape before her, like spring.
Unworthy, I will admit—what blush? who was hurt?
I heard his step and stepped back enduring.
She is gone. A part of someone's life. Perversion
Of such moments: dreams, and divisions of my life
Into before and after, my past a most faithful wife."

May Such Deception Dismay

Until she died from the stress of it all Brahms carried on his affair with his best friend's wife, lying "through the teeth," as the Germans say, letting the world think what it would. His requiem gained a piquancy, the excitement of the forbidden flaunted; "Oh Clara, how could you!" he would say to himself, glass in hand, as he watched her stumble homeward toward Robert in the washed-out light of another morning, her figure foreshortened into dumpiness by the view from his third-floor window. It was all so abstract, and in its way, such a bore.

Longing for the Present

"A creosoted pole on my property, twenty wires cross there in the corner of my back yard—but beyond the wires against the dark clouds (not all clouds are dark) the swallows swoop devouring mosquitoes (assume they eat mosquitoes) and beyond them the tattered, no, the boiling edge of weather moves across me—it was such a view of ice-age glaciers moving—if you look straight up—for a few moments, minutes only, the setting sun gives texture and molecular ambiguity to the utility pole, it glows on the western side—and the neighbor's trees their peculiar shade of green leaning into the light—it was Claude Lorraine—it is lower-middle class here, it is the world. I live for this.

The clouds mean it will rain but I love the sound of my little lawn sprinkler I will keep it going even if it rains this luxury I insist on I live here.

The tattered edge, that cloud assembling itself boiling itself over again assembling its insouciant dissolving grandeur, deliberate, austere, transgressive cloud. The light will never be just this again, was always this, this
is only light."

Keeping House

And for the house he made windows of narrow lights
And against the wall of the house he built chambers round about, against the walls of the house round about, both of the temple and of the oracle: and he made chambers round about:

". . . and the house, when it was in building, was built of stone made ready before it was brought thither: so that there was neither hammer nor axe nor any tool of iron heard in the house, while it was in building."

I Kings: 6

Just As If It Mattered

The child was not talented
would not speak would not listen
would draw incessantly a pigeon
the same pigeon the same view over
and over, a kind of perfection performing
a subtle gray a light silence.

In Case of a Future

"Once in a sycamore I was glad
all at the top, and I sang."

                    John Berryman

Having a Past

Mary, the Virgin, encompassed God
held Him whole if inchoate—
I held Him in my closed mouth—I believed it so—
He never was but He lay there
in the folds of flesh softer than pillows
behind the sexual apertures
serene in hot grottoes.

Glittery

And there are birds in the air
And in the trees.

Forbidden

It is so sad, it is morning.
To the cynical all is theory after all.

Everything Returns

Here I go: he thought. Again
For instance,
American embedded glittery
in the German. *Sprechst du?*
Hours pass; he remembers kissing a woman:

Does It Lose in Translation?

Here, I thought: I am again.
Again, I am here. Beneath her.
Here her hand is. A person has blood
and look how dense the flesh, you can't
pass your hand through it it touches.

Can It Change?

The language of patterns—my mother cutting paper,
Vogue, patterns of paper
dolls soon to be erotically charged: against
Faith, Hope, Charity, Lethargy.

Event is the adventure of the moment:
for example, for adventure at home,
there is dining, turning flesh into flesh,
munching on piteous wounds

                                        Pythagoras.

But Who Speaks?

We say ourselves in syllables that rise
From the floor, rising in speech we do not speak

Wallace Stevens, "The Creations of Sound"

Accidental Childhood

I call it luck when a bird's shadow touches me.

It is hard to know things. "Hard" as in the turtle's
shell, the feel of pebbles in the mouth or pocket.

"Every touch is a modified blow."

Crawley

People believe birds carry danger, disease;
the feel of feathers unlike any other.

Little animals cross frequently the backyard.
Sometimes they die—sparrows, a squirrel; once,
a cat. Good children would bury them
in appropriate boxes. A hummingbird fits
into a matchbox. The shimmer of its throat, as if cut—
the hollyhocks are a mess, but if there's another
bud which might open, let's leave them.

"Man stands erect, he alone, yet he lays him down, stretched out quietly for
sleep, for love, for death—"

Hermann Broch, *The Death of Virgil*

And what child does not suffer silent and alone? That's
what it means, "child"— a problem and a pathos. Like
Latin the words ran, like chocolate in summer: "How do you
suppose the Romans spoke?" the teacher said, her eyes
unfocused, having said it all already: (Eye, a room—ease as east.)

49

Mortal Danger: Funerary Art

Zeroing a life like that aiming
and poof you're dead. Dear me.
The weight of bodies the way they churn
under there—take the long view.
Now. Then. And I notice the sky is blue
just as her paintings show, and clouds
clouds do stutter across then fade
into the mountains which appear
transparent in this light. Trust the season.

All through the ceremony birds
would coalesce among the trees
swerve once a gracious curve
whitish against the various greens
then be gone. Then they'd
do it again. Trees are their own terror.

The terrible transparency of stone.
I love sparrows most, the grayest small
least lovable—they come to this table arrogant
in hunger balancing fear against failed
nature—awaiting demanding not begging
crumbs from us—never a friend, and a life
months long, several seasons, then
over (the trouble is, if you sit long
enough, the sparrows become distinguishable,
individual, ones of a kind, doomed)
if you arrange the possibilities
you can see the shape of air—clouds or
just the intensity of the blue. Clouds.
Always motion. A place to live, a way.

A cormorant inches above the surface
snaking double trail of swirls where wing tips
touch or just the wind touches spots on the water
circles the lake completely then returns
to the very branch—it seems a sheer
exuberance of skill but is perhaps the desperation
of hunger who can tell who is not that bird

his poetry hers the amazing long neck
the wings' rhythm the color like a military trio
of cormorants preening

two more come perform this one turning
touches the water their serpentine slenderness

two men also fishing bundled against
the spring cold each attends two rods propped
against the rocks the passivity a kind
of morality the birds' aggression beautiful
or whose patience is better more beautiful
a kind of beauty a sin the sunlight
begins to sharpen shadows now
coalesce on this page the shadows
the nib of my pen appears making
its dance along the lines the lined guides

the green the grass and trees no meaning
the contortions of limbs are painful to consider
but is how they are almost who

the wake spreading a ceremonial veil
behind two ducks approaching me—
the wakes cross—and above them
the cormorants—no wind—the lines
of force a terrific geometry.

Leibniz said that music is a secret
arithmetical ability of the mind
that does not know it is
counting do birds hear music?

There are nine cormorants crossing
the pond, they darken the horizon
they balance themselves
they eat fish they shit in the water
their necks evolved this way.

A sphere is a kind of perfection so
is a cipher a zero whiteness of page
or fearful face a bondage of absence
fullness of time emptiness of gesture
a geometry of agonies. Anything.

On the Shape of Such as Planets, Like Earth

Light expands spherically—fanciful dandelion,
rays and dots, waves and particles—the match lighted and
in half a second a sphere a hundred-eighty-six-
thousand miles in diameter except for the shadows—
a pearl of universe, a place to play to be

this morning in this city the wash of light, the angle
of sunlight is thirty-five degrees—estimate from watching
the old men chase their slow shadows westward
while the young walk north to south, south
to north, their shadows beside them tucked among
the walls and windows—the city threatens

the fyn perl congeleth and wexeth gret of the dew of heuene.
                              ·Mandeville's *Travels*, chap. xiv, f. 65 b

as silver cars swim downstream to the light
then stop. Then start. The buses bellow. The light.
Changes. The sky. A different smell. A scratching
inside the lung of light, inside the eye, against
the cornea. The long morning fills.

And how ridiculous my sight I wipe my eyes
my vision I breathe deeply of a heron stalking
his legs hinged backward his spear-beak
poised even the glitter of his great eye stilled
to more stealthily stalk oh mercy and good-
ness shall follow me.

God, a sphere, round, rejoicing in solitude.
                              Empedocles, Book 1, frag. 135

Pearl is also a color of sky, mother of pearl also.
It hatches in the dark wet oyster it is a daughter
of light of contradiction. Pearl is the shape of rain

and the city shimmers today shivers in gray light
it is a house to kings and counselors of the earth, which
built desolate places for themselves (Job 3: 14).

As for the earth, out of it cometh bread, and under it
is turned up as it were fire.
The stones of it are the place of sapphires:
and it hath dust of gold
he said. But what of the light, and then
there are pearls, which rest upon the breasts
of the lovely, and the languishing, and the breath
goes in and out and the pearl warms, and the mother
of pearl is a light laughter, a longing.

Riches and anything that shape the shape
of the earth itself the globe the shape delights
and instructs. The light glints. The shadow
hovers. The bird was once the shape of the egg.
The roundness of anything redeems. And the light.
The fish that makes a pearl at low tide opens
and receives the dew, the stuff of pearls—
it could be so, it was, or was believed,
Congealed dew. The glitter of seawater streaming
off the knobbed and gnarled back of the oyster
the lesson is too wrong for any to resist,
inner versus outer, books and covers
and who would eat will eat and swallow light.

How Various It Is and Quiet

How Lonely

The speaking of a syllable is another chapter
in the history of silence there is no silence
history is noise   words
wobble onward singing of decay—
quarters spun on a zinc bar—who cares
these days about the law   second of
thermodynamics   has it been repealed
I could not have been more than nine
years old the first time I saw
the glitter of glassware in the high window
of the high school's laboratory—
there was a deep alley from the playground
I passed that way daily the high window-
sill where beakers and flasks aligned in light
would shimmer and did I or only dream
I climbed the wall and peered in expensively
where Bunsen burners votively ranged
themselves beside cool waters chasubles
hung on hooks white coats   there is
no silence the world wobbles
softly

          Pleasure is a word.
There are no differences there are only
differences (see Keats). Tremble (see
leaves; see lips, see drops, as of water,
tears, titration fluids held by the skillfully
stopped pipette) and it is a world. The air
trembles. The dogs in the street tremble.
The street trembles. Now.
             The world
is surface: to penetrate surface
is to create more surface. Live with it.
Take, for instance, art.

I will draw his drawings again. I
will paint his paintings. Paint is
a new surface. There is only one
surface and it covers Reality forever
in every direction See you can see it
Look you can touch it Touch you
are it. Be. The high school had a high
window and I tried to see
through it. I could see it
from where I stood on the earth.
Trembling. There was a word for it.

In the darkened room a print by Torii
Kiyomitsu done oh two hundred years
ago Chasing Fireflies the single female
figure tries to bat them down
with her fan the wind flings her
kimono dangerously aside the
plaque on the wall says Dangerously
Erotic   the poem in the upper   *the calligraphy includes*
right corner says Firefly, firefly, come   *twisted lines which*
this way here is the path to love   *are the fireflies*
her leg is long she is surface, ink,   *depicted*
the skin of the woman is paper
the uninked surface the untouched surface
which trembles. Her thigh does not tremble.
We love her like science
while we live.

Dumb Cake

they meet in silence and at twelve oclock they eat it still silent for if one speaks the
spell is broken when they have done they walk up to bed backwards and those
that are to be married see the likeness of their sweet hearts hurrying after them

John Clare

There is no sweetness like the future.
There is no future.

I will calculate my days my fortune on the change in my pocket, She
loves me she loves me not, tossing the coins as counted onto the
sidewalk not noticing as children follow me picking up the glittering
detritus; *calculate* means stone, not coin.

For a long time I used to sleep late
and then one morning an angel appeared to me
a weeping angel behind glass motioning
slowly to me, signaling solemnly
to make me laugh

The leaves do quiver on this tree, the one outside my window, in the sun and
cold—their number is countable, but pointless. Still, it is the sort of thing one
wonders: how many leaves on an average size aspen, how many on a beech, live oak,
is the number odd or even by the time you finish counting you are wrong leaves
have fallen others have unfolded oh look a butterfly this late and this high, the
twelfth floor does it feel the cold can it count the hours left in its life?

If there is a life after this one it does not matter there is no reward for goodness no
punishment for evil—no one blames the butterfly for the ravages of the caterpillar.

Give us this day our dailiness.

Removing her last vestige, her last
vestment which took infinitely long to
fall just down just twisting to tie itself into a knot,
to tie itself that little wisp of rayon
into something, some leaf rising on wind
in transition egg
to adult, some winged vision. Some theatrical
machinery the light what light there is thick
and music behind it all like the movies
soft music and sirens. Sadness
when the season changes and children grow
bold again, then history has begun.

Next to Nothing

There was a man suffered the severance
of his penis—an absence made public and
it made him a star
of the pornographic magazines
he could arouse curiosity.

He who desires something is in want of
something; he who desires nothing
       is in want of nothing   Socrates (Plato, *The Symposium*)

            Writing implies the absence of the writer   Anne Carson

He who desires writing desires the absence
of the writer; he who is in want of a writer
is in want of nothing; writing resolves itself
rewards nothing.

death—whispers softly
    —I am no one—   Mallarmé (Paul Auster),
                                             A Tomb for Anatole

The absence filled the fertile imagination—
everyone wants to see nothing
to know how it feels if
it feels, if there is surer silence
in the flesh if one can be so quiet there and yet live

the world as lived in is a type of betrayal
language vibrates with the need and nearness of espionage
nothing is harder than knowing. . . .

this man, his wife made him famous and flesh she knew
and the flesh which was his was sleeping—
a sharp knife a shadow

there was, no doubt, blood, and a trial after
and he had beaten her and her suffering led her
to remove the cause and husband / wife knowledge
is sweet and does the earth speak to itself through
flesh this way it is what love means to the soft earth
if it is not a dream
it might have been a dream

                    the tender flesh hardens
with time and touch

             writing is not speech / absence "writing
implies the absence of the author" speech flowers
like blood from the wound there is never anything
to say, not only between husbands and wives and fathers
and sons and daughters and mothers   Mother implies
absence of the Father   etc.

                Some nights ago I woke
and from my high window in the city saw
white clouds low against a black sky
with stars if I had walked through
that window I would have stepped
out of flesh who might have followed

no child knows better. Absence. Words
are a spy upon interiority   into
our simple closed selves
silence a strict master
the only comfort   touchingly
I cannot pronounce the words the world
hears my mistakes and knows me for what
I am   what sound did he make
like a severed tongue the small flesh
                    lay dying
                        Ah Philomel

If a man is a museum of failed ambitions
a grave to his own childhood is a woman?
                              I know a woman

I know a woman whose husband died in a hospital
a television high on the wall not like a window
like a cage a cube and electrical
and the other man in the room would not
turn it off the sound loud and thin   the death
continued it was a modern death drowned
by laughter and light the light of a kind
of heaven   glass light and immortality

he was a sculptor and made his art of steel
and glass   he is still dead

        tears—
        simply remain
        not to <u>touch</u>
        but to speak—

Mallarmé (Paul Auster),
A Tomb for Anatole

Oh, it is not nothing to die, nor to live.
It is soft speaking.

String

The new theory of the universe predicts,
for instance, gravity. And history. It is correct.
It is complex. There are men too eager to know,
and women. And nothing succeeds like it,
success as historical accident. An image
of impudence, a kind of catastrophe:
Pluck. Thrum. Strum. Pizzicato physics.
The body suffers more for its own sake than
for the mind, the mind complains. Here we make
beautiful music, here we are together. Think
about it, and tremble. It is a wonder the world
wobbles forward with us on it, riding in our
howdahs, happy too often, bleeding careless
into the rivers. (*Howdah*, from the Arabic,
to totter, as if on the back of an elephant
to sway and threaten disaster, like the earth
and humanity, humankind, people, tribes
and tribulations, races and rants, man and woman,
like the sun and its faithful planet, earth,
leashed by gravity, or so the new theory
predicts, out for its exercise, wobbly
full of beans, or of the past, particles and hadrons
and bright little dots of mu mesons whirling,
flealike and jumpy. This earth. You remember.)
It looks like rain. But is really a star
fallen, full into the neighborhood. It looks
bad for the future, but is really the past.
Many of us feared it would end this way.
It is wicked. The birds fly carefully around it.
It was formerly known as the future but is
now called the past. Or so we must assume,
just to be safe. We live this way.
Her hair thick with music lies
on me. Each time is the first. Consider
that she now predicts gravity, her theory

an art: an accident of history makes her young.
Her skin is paper and her eyes are ink.
There is no note she cannot be, no need.
Music is something she might die of, or art or
that other mathematics, the one that predicts
the end of everything.

Trouble Deaf Heaven

Sonnet 29

Is there a sound? There is a forest.
What is the world? The word is wilderness.
What is the answer? The answer is the world.
What is the beginning? A beginning is happiness.
What is the end? No one lives there now.
What is a beginning? The beginning is light.
What makes happiness? Nothing.
What makes an ending? What does not.
What is her skin? *Her skin is composed of strange clothing and clouds of butterflies,*
of events and odors, of the rose fingers of dawn, transparent suns of full
daylight, blue loves of dusk and night fish with huge eyes.

Max Walter Svanberg

What makes a question? Birds in the evening.
When do birds die? When it is complete.
What makes a world? The leaves shimmer in the wind, they
reverberate with small heat and large wind and they cannot be counted.
What is music? A man lives there with his sister, they count the buses passing
their window, and they count the small-winged insects which die on that
windowsill.
Who is happy? Nothing is necessary, everything that is is.
When does it end? *A green delight the wounded mind endears*
After the hustling world is broken off.

John Clare

What is the beginning? The completion.
How does it complicate? In that it dazzles.
When does it matter? Blue loaves of dusk.
What perishes?
Who listens? There will be prizes.
What is a child? Blue lives of dusk.
Where does dust come from? From tropical skies.
When is it over? *. . . into childhood . . . into fantasy . . . through the streets of New*
York . . . through tropical skies . . . into the receiving trays the balls come to rest
releasing prizes.

Joseph Cornell

63

What does a child do? Listens with his body, with her body.
When does it end? Listens with the hands.
Does it end? The hands which are small and wide.
Where do children come from? White pebbles.
Who suffers? No one returns from there.
Who suffers? There was once a small forest with a path of white pebbles
       and a tame group of frights and follies; whoever entered knew
       the path would carry them to the other side, but that it would be
       scary and fun at the same time. No one who entered was ever seen again.
Is there a sound? There is a forest.
Who listens? The large lady with the small dog, she leans into the
       neighbor's yard to sniff the hydrangea once more hoping
       this time it will have an odor, a sweetness which she feels
       such a desperate need for she is near despair, she is thinking
       of killing herself except who would care for the dog, who could know
       what he feels what he needs what his smelly bed in the corner actually
       means to him.
What matters? There is a forest.
Who listens? Another theory of the origin of the universe holds that
       "matter" is a way of thinking, a little like love, actually, if you think
       of it that way.
What matters? There is a forest.
What is the word? There is color, and no one knows what to do with it.
       We would be happier without it is one theory; we are irresponsible
       and full of angers like colors.
What does the child think? The child.
What does the child think? Happiness.
What child? A word is a small part of itself, it is round at times, and it satisfies
       only itself.
Does it answer? It does not.
What is pain? A small island, or perhaps it is a large island, the adjective is
       merely relative and a convenience. There are few inhabitants—one,
       actually, ever at a time—and the sky's red would perhaps be beautiful if
       there were another even a single other inhabitant, alas.
What is pain? A man turns and locks his door with exactly the same small
       dance of hands every morning at the same hour and pockets the key
       followed by a pat of the pocket with the hand which just locked the
       door. Unknown to him it is his life, it is the center and source of what
       he calls his life. It makes him what he is happy to call happy.

Who suffers? Oh, it is true, there are causes of cruelty, it is that kind of world.
What is geometry? It is how we know, and what.
What is the purpose of memory? Blue lines of dust.
What is the cat when she yawns?
What is dust?
Does the child suffer? The child is suffering.
Is the child cruel? The child crushes the world at will, the child destroys
      with angelic decorum, the child bleeds into his own drinking water
      and smiles to see color a demon and delirium the child is born knowing
      and screaming and there is pain in his fist when he enters and there is
      pain as if the atoms which whirl mad in their completeness were tiny
      childbirths and it is the cruelty of children which presses upon the
      innocent earth and coal turns to diamond.
What is to perish?
What is to choose?
What is to crush?

Gravity and Levity

Where assassins sleep a wash
of dream breaks against bars

hours of every day are night
a furious freedom a breath

a humid flight returning to
serious childhoods—what else is

dream—enactment and revenge
the released terrors swirl

every rapist in sleep renews
his first fond wish to kiss and kill

and is a secret self. Does she make
music from that body? I see she

is bruised she played herself hard
or someone did. She has bled

she has a bandaged body; she is lovely
does she love me as I slip the dollars in

the slot above the window
where the faint sound wisps?

No one is sadder. She is bruised
(who is not?) she loved

the world didn't know better
she lived there. A voice

settles, a sheet spun
out over the bed settles

under air, in, through, air, weight
the weight of voice settles

on, into the bed. You are lying
unclothed, perhaps cold

waiting to be wanted
it will talk you into something like

being warm at night. Or the air
on the air, the breath a kindness floats

the breath is air it floats in air, air
of your air—take and breathe

this is my breath—it takes the shape
of what it settles on, who listens.

Who speaks too soon too often.
The great democracy of flesh—

all are guilty. All sleep.
In German, a language,

the art of heaviness is called *schwerkraft,*

                                                gravity

O heavy the little body hers;

"But from the sleeper falls,   *Doch aus dem Schlafenden fallt,*
as though from a still cloud,   *wie aus lagernder Wolke,*

the opulent rain of the grave."   *reichlicher Regen der Schwere.*
Make sense of the world, do not resist

the ready term. Well, welcome the rising
and falling. I was a happy boy who placed

the coins in the ready slots. Eyes. I watched
the dance I felt the rising. The eyes

closed a little, O, a heaviness of the lids,
like little caskets closed.

O and again O.
In 1612 John Donne wrote in response

to the blush of a lady, "her body thinks"—
(of Elizabeth Drury, "The Second Anniversary")

a trick how curves of space have
their way with the body the boiling

of the particles defying: delirious
damage accruing

live in landscape a place
where it rains clouds rise

to make home (long for days
of decorum and starlight)

the body thinks and the body's
thought inscribes itself abrasion

welt   weal   lesion   scar
bruise   freckle   pimple

postule   pride   boil   wart and mole and
malignancy   abscess   wound,   O.

5. In all things there is a portion of everything
except mind; and there are things in which
there is mind too.

17. The Greeks do not rightly use the terms
"coming into being" and "perishing."
For nothing comes into being nor yet
does anything perish, but there is mixture
and separation of things that are.
So they would do right in calling
the coming into being "mixture,"
and the perishing "separation."

18. For how could hair come from what is not hair?
Or flesh from what is not flesh?

Anaxagoras

The heron resolves itself from the gray lake the water
conversely the woman dissolves in sex, her own

in liquefaction but the flesh reforms like wings
unfolded flight like light drips glistens

the setting sun the horizon first
above now below the bird the evening only local

the spinning earth flings its fluid surface
dissolving itself into itself its ecstasy

the need we feel each for each, the falseness
of any world, at all it is a kind of patience

impossible to distinguish from lassitude
it is a kind of hope indistinguishable

from stupidity. I know (of) a man who killed
himself and the woman he was about to marry

killed herself a month later. He wrote a note:
Until yesterday I had no definite plan to kill myself.

I do not understand it myself, but it is not
because of a particular event, nor of an explicit matter.

Every elliptic curve defined over the rational field
is a factor of the Jacobian of a modular function field

was another note he wrote. (I have his picture
on my desk, a gray parallelogram,

a thin man in black jacket black
tie bifurcating a horizon behind him

the line just above his ears this point
of view this lonely life there is only

a kind of barrenness in the background and a sky
which is a world, of course, plenty.)

This is a bigger world than it was once
it expands an explosion it can't help it it has

nothing to do with us with whether we know or
not whether our theories can be proved

whether or not a mathematician
knew a better class of circles

(he has a name, Taniyama, a Conjecture)
than was ever known before before—

not circles, elliptic curves. Not doughnuts.
Not anything that is nearly, only is, such

a world is hard to imagine, harder to live in,
harder still to leave. A little like love, Dear.